FINANCIAL INTELLIGENCE
FOR KIDS

A Guide for Teaching Kids Skills of
Money Making, Multiplying and
Managing

STEX STEPHEN

TABLE OF CONTENT

INTRODUCTION

In the vibrant town of Prosperityville, there lived a group of curious and ambitious children eager to understand the mysteries of money. Their journey into the realm of financial intelligence began when they stumbled upon a remarkable guide titled **"Financial Intelligence for Kids"**.

In this enchanting guide, the children discovered a world where dollars and cents were not mere pieces of paper but keys to unlocking a lifetime of possibilities. The guide aimed to empower young minds with the knowledge and skills necessary to navigate the complex landscape of personal finance.

The heart of the guide lay in its collaborative approach involving parents and educators. As the children absorbed the wisdom from the guide, they began to witness positive changes in their lives. They learned to make informed choices, set financial goals, and develop a healthy relationship with money. The once-mysterious world of finance transformed into a playground of opportunities, where each child could shape their financial destiny.

In Prosperityville, **"Financial Intelligence for Kids"** written by **Stex Stephen**, became a cherished resource for families and schools alike. It sparked a financial revolution, empowering a new generation with the tools to make sound financial decisions. The children of Prosperityville grew up with not just a pocket full of coins but with the invaluable gift of financial intelligence—a treasure that would serve them well throughout their lives.

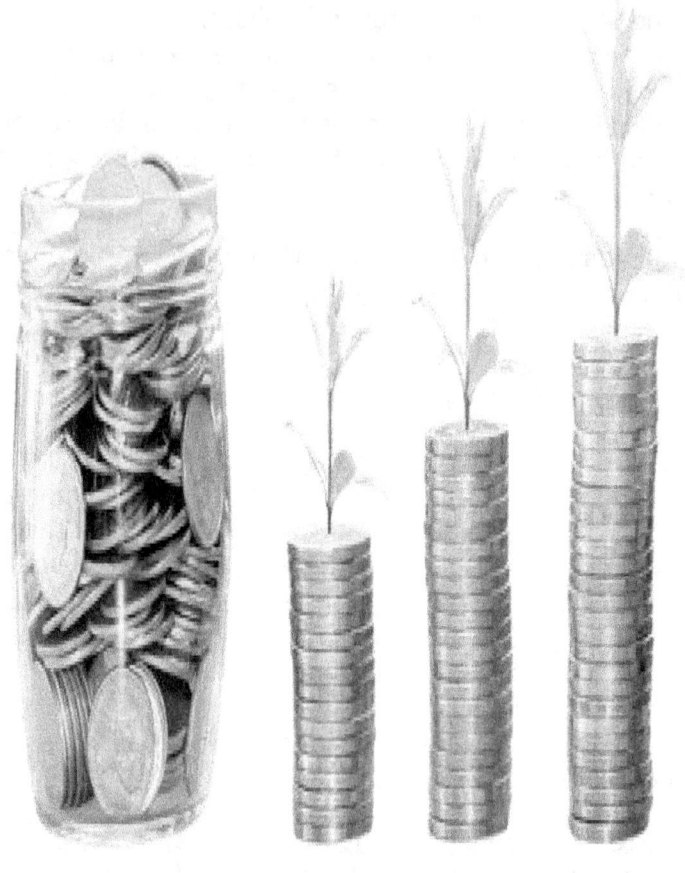

CHAPTER ONE

UNDERSTANDING THE BASICS OF MONEY FOR KIDS

What is Money?

Money is a multifaceted and indispensable instrument that permeates every aspect of modern economic life, serving as a medium of exchange, unit of account, and store of value. At its core, money is a social construct, a system of symbols and agreed-upon conventions that facilitate the complex web of transactions and economic interactions within a society. The evolution of money reflects the dynamic nature of human societies and their economic structures.

The fundamental purpose of money is to overcome the limitations of barter, where goods and services were exchanged directly for one another. Barter systems were inherently inefficient, as the double coincidence of wants—requiring both parties to have something the other desired—was a significant obstacle. Money emerged as a solution to this problem, providing a universally accepted medium that could facilitate transactions between disparate individuals and communities.

Money takes various forms, each with its own characteristics and historical origins. Commodity money, such as gold or silver, has intrinsic value and has been used throughout history as a medium of exchange. Representative money, on the other hand, is backed by a physical commodity but is not the commodity itself; examples include paper currency redeemable for a specific amount of precious metal. Fiat money, the most prevalent form today, has no intrinsic value and derives its worth from the trust and confidence of the people who use it.

Central to the concept of money is its role as a store of value. Money allows individuals to save and defer consumption, enabling them to accumulate wealth over time. This function is crucial for economic development, as it provides the financial stability necessary for long-term planning and investment. However, the value of money can be influenced by external factors such as inflation, economic instability, or changes in the global financial landscape.

As a unit of account, money serves as a common measure of value for goods and services. This function facilitates economic calculation, allowing individuals and businesses to compare the relative worth of different items and make informed decisions about resource allocation. The unit of account function is essential for establishing prices, creating a basis for contracts, and fostering a standardized system of economic measurement.

The evolution of money has seen a transition from physical forms to digital and virtual representations. In the modern era, electronic transactions, cryptocurrencies, and digital payment systems have become integral components of the monetary landscape. These innovations offer convenience, speed, and accessibility, but they also pose challenges related to privacy, security, and regulatory frameworks.

The concept of money is a dynamic and multifaceted phenomenon that has evolved throughout human history in response to the changing needs and complexities of economic interactions. Whether in the form of coins, banknotes, digital bits, or cryptocurrencies, money continues to play a central role in shaping the economic and social structures of societies worldwide. Understanding the nature of money is essential for navigating the intricate web of financial relationships that define the modern global economy.

The History of Money
The history of money is a fascinating chronicle that mirrors the evolution of human civilization and economic systems. From the barter

exchanges of ancient societies to the sophisticated digital transactions of the modern era, the concept of money has undergone a remarkable transformation. This journey through time unveils the pivotal moments and diverse forms that money has taken, illustrating its profound impact on societies and shaping the course of human history.

Barter and Early Forms of Exchange: In the early stages of human civilization, people engaged in barter, exchanging goods and services directly. While this system facilitated basic transactions, its limitations became evident as societies grew more complex. The inefficiencies and impracticalities of barter paved the way for the emergence of primitive forms of money, such as cowrie shells, salt, and even livestock, which held intrinsic value and served as a medium of exchange.

The Birth of Coinage: The ancient civilizations of Mesopotamia, Egypt, and Greece marked a significant shift with the introduction of metal coins. These standardized units of currency, typically made from precious metals like gold or silver, streamlined trade and eliminated some of the challenges associated with barter. The widespread use of coins fostered economic growth, enabling more extensive commerce and the accumulation of wealth.

Paper Money and Banking: As societies continued to advance, the need for a more flexible medium of exchange led to the development of paper money. China, in the 7th century, is credited with issuing the first known paper currency. This innovation gained traction worldwide, with European nations adopting paper money in the later centuries. Concurrently, the establishment of banks and the issuance of banknotes further revolutionized financial systems, providing a convenient alternative to heavy metal coins.

The Gold Standard and Modern Banking: The 19th century witnessed the dominance of the gold standard, where currencies were directly tied to a specific quantity of gold. This system aimed to provide stability and prevent excessive inflation. However, the constraints of the gold standard became apparent during times of economic turmoil, leading to its eventual abandonment in the 20th century. The rise of central banking and fiat currencies ushered in a new era, allowing governments to control and regulate the money supply independently of precious metal reserves.

Digital Money and Cryptocurrencies: In the 21st century, the landscape of money underwent another revolution with the advent of digital currencies. Cryptocurrencies, such as Bitcoin and Ethereum, emerged as decentralized and secure alternatives to traditional forms of money. Blockchain technology, the backbone of cryptocurrencies, introduced a transparent and tamper-resistant ledger, challenging established financial systems and prompting discussions about the future of money in the digital age.

The history of money is a dynamic tapestry woven through the fabric of human civilization, reflecting the changing needs, technologies, and economic structures of societies. From humble beginnings in barter systems to the complex financial instruments of today, the journey of money is an ongoing saga that continues to shape the course of global economies and influence the way we interact, trade, and build our shared future.

Types of Money

Money, in its various forms, serves as a fundamental medium of exchange, unit of account, and store of value within economic systems. The evolution of money has witnessed a fascinating journey from ancient barter systems to modern digital currencies. Different forms of money have emerged over time, reflecting the needs and advancements of societies.

One of the earliest forms of money was commodity money, where items with intrinsic value, such as gold, silver, or precious stones, were used as a medium of exchange. This system provided a tangible and universally accepted measure of value, fostering trade and economic development. However, carrying and securing physical commodities posed challenges.

As societies progressed, representative money emerged, backed by a tangible asset but represented by a more convenient form, like paper currency or coins. This allowed for easier transactions and reduced the risks associated with handling precious metals. The shift towards representative money marked a pivotal moment in the history of monetary systems.

In the modern era, fiat money has become the predominant form of currency. Unlike commodity or representative money, fiat currency does not have intrinsic value and is not backed by a physical commodity. Instead, its value is derived from the trust and confidence of the people using it. Governments issue fiat currency and regulate its circulation, aiming to maintain stability and control over the economy.

In recent decades, digital currencies have emerged as a revolutionary form of money. Cryptocurrencies, such as Bitcoin and Ethereum, operate on decentralized blockchain technology. These digital assets offer increased security, transparency, and borderless transactions, challenging traditional notions of currency and financial systems. The rise of digital currencies has sparked debates about their impact on traditional banking and monetary policies.

Furthermore, the concept of central bank digital currencies (CBDCs) has gained traction, with some countries exploring the issuance of digital versions of their national currencies. CBDCs aim to combine the benefits of traditional fiat currency with the efficiency of digital transactions, potentially transforming the landscape of global finance.

The concept of money has evolved over time, adapting to the changing needs and complexities of human societies. From commodity money to fiat currency and the advent of digital currencies, each form of money reflects the technological, economic, and social advancements of its era. The ongoing exploration of new forms, such as digital and central bank-issued currencies, underscores the dynamic nature of money in the contemporary world.

CHAPTER TWO

THE IMPORTANCE OF FINANCIAL EDUCATION FOR KIDS

Why is Financial Education Crucial?

Financial education is a crucial aspect of a child's development that equips them with the knowledge and skills necessary to navigate the complex world of money. In an era where financial decisions play a significant role in shaping one's future, instilling financial literacy in children from an early age is more important than ever.

One of the primary reasons why financial education is crucial for kids is that it lays the foundation for a lifetime of responsible money management. By teaching children about basic financial concepts such as budgeting, saving, and investing, we empower them to make informed decisions about their finances as they grow older. This early exposure helps cultivate responsible spending habits, fostering a sense of financial discipline that will serve them well throughout their lives.

Moreover, financial education provides children with the tools to navigate an increasingly complex financial landscape. As the world becomes more interconnected, individuals are faced with a myriad of financial choices, from choosing the right credit card to understanding the implications of loans and mortgages. By arming children with the knowledge to decipher financial jargon and comprehend the consequences of their choices, we empower them to make sound financial decisions that align with their long-term goals.

Beyond the practical aspects, financial education also cultivates a sense of financial confidence and independence. Children who understand the value of money and the importance of financial planning are more likely to approach financial challenges with resilience and resourcefulness. This confidence not only prepares them for the financial responsibilities of adulthood but also instills a sense of empowerment, enabling them to take control of their financial destinies.

Furthermore, in a world where economic landscapes are constantly evolving, financial education fosters adaptability. Children equipped with financial knowledge are better prepared to navigate economic uncertainties, whether it be changes in employment opportunities, fluctuations in the stock market, or unexpected expenses. This adaptability is a valuable life skill that goes beyond financial matters, influencing their overall ability to tackle challenges and embrace change.

In conclusion, financial education for kids is not merely about dollars and cents; it is an investment in their future well-being. By providing children with the tools to make informed financial decisions, we empower them to achieve financial stability, independence, and resilience. As we prepare the next generation for the complexities of the modern world, ensuring that they are financially literate becomes an integral part of equipping them for success in all facets of life.

How Early Financial Education Benefits Children

As societies become increasingly complex, instilling a strong foundation of financial knowledge in children has emerged as a critical aspect of their overall education. Early financial education not only equips children with practical skills for managing money but also cultivates a mindset that fosters responsible financial behavior in adulthood. In this passage, we delve into the multifaceted benefits of providing children with a solid financial education, exploring how it empowers them to navigate the complexities of the modern financial landscape.

Development of Money Management Skills: One of the primary advantages of early financial education lies in its ability to develop fundamental money management skills in children. By introducing concepts such as budgeting, saving, and spending wisely at a young age, children learn to appreciate the value of money and understand the consequences of their financial decisions. These skills form the building blocks for responsible financial behavior, setting the stage for a lifetime of sound fiscal management.

Cultivation of Financial Responsibility: Early financial education fosters a sense of financial responsibility in children, teaching them to make informed choices about money from an early age. As they grasp the concept of earning, saving, and spending, children develop an awareness of the consequences of their financial decisions. This early exposure to financial responsibility lays the groundwork for prudent financial habits in adulthood, reducing the likelihood of falling into debt or making impulsive financial choices.

Enhancement of Critical thinking and Problem Solving Skills: Financial education is not merely about numbers; it also plays a pivotal role in enhancing critical thinking and problem-solving skills in children. As they grapple with real-world financial scenarios, such as creating a budget or setting financial goals, children learn to analyze situations, make informed decisions, and solve problems creatively. These cognitive skills are transferable to various aspects of their lives, contributing to their overall academic and personal development.

Prevention of Financial Illiteracy: The global rise in financial complexities underscores the urgency of addressing financial illiteracy. Early financial education acts as a preventive measure, arming children with the knowledge and skills needed to navigate the intricate financial landscape they will encounter as adults. By instilling a strong financial foundation, educators and parents alike can empower the next generation to make sound financial choices, thereby mitigating the risks associated with financial illiteracy.

Long Term impact on Financial Well Being: The impact of early financial education extends far beyond childhood and adolescence. Studies consistently show that individuals with a solid financial education are more likely to achieve financial stability and success in adulthood. From making informed investment decisions to planning for major life events like homeownership and retirement, the long-term benefits of early financial education contribute significantly to an individual's overall financial well-being.

Early financial education is an invaluable investment in the future success and well-being of our children. By equipping them with essential money management skills, fostering financial responsibility, and promoting critical thinking, we empower the next generation to navigate the complexities of the modern financial world with confidence and competence. As we recognize the profound impact of early financial education, it becomes clear that preparing children for financial success is not just an educational imperative but a societal responsibility.

CHAPTER THREE

SETTING THE FOUNDATION: TEACHING KIDS ABOUT SAVING

The Concept of Saving

In the journey of raising children, imparting essential life skills goes beyond academic education. One crucial aspect that often takes a backseat in traditional curricula is financial literacy. Introducing the concept of saving to kids at an early age lays the foundation for responsible money management and fosters a sense of financial independence.

Teaching children the value of saving is akin to providing them with a powerful tool that will serve them well throughout their lives. By instilling this habit from a young age, parents and caregivers can help shape a positive attitude towards money and financial responsibility.

At its core, the concept of saving for kids revolves around instilling discipline and patience. Children are naturally inclined to want instant gratification, but teaching them to delay immediate desires for future gains is a valuable lesson. This not only encourages self-control but also helps build resilience, a vital trait in navigating life's challenges.

Parents can start by introducing the basics of money through hands-on experiences. Using piggy banks or clear jars, children can visually see the accumulation of their savings over time. This tangible representation provides a concrete understanding of the connection between saving and achieving goals, whether it's for a coveted toy or a future endeavour.

Moreover, involving kids in discussions about financial goals as a family promotes open communication and transparency. Explaining the concept of short-term and long-term goals allows children to understand the importance of budgeting and prioritizing their wants and needs. As they grow, this early exposure to financial decision-making will empower them to make informed choices as adults.

In a world increasingly driven by consumerism, teaching kids about saving also equips them with the ability to differentiate between needs and wants. By guiding them through decisions about spending, parents contribute to the development of a conscious and mindful approach to money.

Introducing the concept of saving for kids is a powerful investment in their future. By nurturing financial literacy from an early age, parents and caregivers provide children with the tools to navigate the complex world of finance responsibly. This not only fosters a sense of independence but also instills values that will contribute to their overall well-being and success in the years to come.

Importance of Savings For Kids

Teaching children about financial responsibility early on is paramount to their future success. One crucial aspect of this financial education is instilling the habit of saving money. The importance of savings for kids goes beyond the simple act of accumulating funds; it lays the foundation for a lifetime of financial well-being and empowerment.

First and foremost, introducing children to the concept of savings helps them develop a sense of discipline and delayed gratification. By setting aside a portion of their allowance or monetary gifts, kids learn that not every desire must be instantly fulfilled. This valuable lesson instills patience and cultivates a mindset that is essential for navigating the complexities of adult financial responsibilities.

Savings also serve as a safety net, teaching children the importance of being prepared for unforeseen circumstances. Whether it's a broken toy, an unexpected expense, or a future investment opportunity, having a savings cushion provides a sense of security and control. Kids learn that financial setbacks are a natural part of life, and having savings empowers them to overcome challenges with confidence.

Furthermore, saving money at a young age fosters the development of goal-setting skills. Whether it's saving for a special toy, a gadget, or even their education, setting specific financial goals encourages children to plan and work towards achieving them. This early exposure to goal-setting lays the groundwork for responsible financial planning in adulthood, helping them navigate larger financial objectives such as buying a home, pursuing higher education, or starting a business.

Teaching kids about the magic of compound interest is another crucial aspect of the importance of savings. By explaining how money grows over time when it's saved, children grasp the concept that their financial choices today can have a significant impact on their future wealth. This knowledge empowers them to make informed decisions about saving and investing, setting the stage for long-term financial success.

The importance of savings for kids extends far beyond the tangible accumulation of money. It is a powerful tool for imparting life skills, cultivating financial responsibility, and fostering a mindset of empowerment. By teaching children the value of saving early on, we equip them with the tools they need to make sound financial decisions, setting the stage for a lifetime of financial well-being and success.

Fun Ways to Encourage Saving

Teaching kids the value of money and the importance of saving from an early age sets the foundation for a lifetime of financial responsibility. While the concept of saving might seem dull to youngsters, incorporating fun and engaging activities can make the learning process enjoyable. Here are some creative and entertaining ways to encourage saving for kids, turning financial education into an exciting adventure.

1. *Personalized Piggy Banks*: Provide each child with a plain piggy bank and let them unleash their creativity by decorating it with stickers, paint, and markers. Personalizing their own piggy bank not only makes saving more exciting but also instills a sense of ownership and pride in their savings efforts.
2. *Goal Setting with Rewards*: Help kids set realistic savings goals, whether it's for a special toy, a day out with friends, or a future treat. Attach a visual representation of their goal to their piggy bank, and each time they save, they move one step closer. Once the goal is reached, celebrate their achievement with a small reward, reinforcing the positive habit of saving.

3. *Saving Jars for Different Purposes*: Introduce the concept of allocating money for different purposes by using saving jars. Label each jar for specific goals such as toys, outings, or even charity. This not only teaches kids about budgeting but also allows them to experience the joy of giving back, fostering a well-rounded understanding of money management.

4. *Interactive Savings Apps*: In the digital age, there are numerous interactive and child-friendly savings apps designed to make money management enjoyable. These apps often include games, challenges, and colorful visuals to engage kids while teaching them about financial concepts such as earning, saving, and spending wisely.

5. *Storytime with Financial Tales*: Incorporate financial lessons into storytime by reading books that revolve around money-related adventures. Choose stories that feature characters learning about the value of saving and making wise financial choices. This approach combines entertainment with education, making the learning experience more relatable for kids.

6. *DIY Savings Thermometer*: Create a savings thermometer by drawing a large thermometer on a poster board. As kids deposit money into their savings, color in

the thermometer to visually represent their progress. This simple yet effective visual aid provides a tangible way for kids to see their savings grow and stay motivated to reach their goals.

Encouraging kids to save money doesn't have to be a tedious task; it can be a fun and rewarding experience. By combining creativity, goal setting, and interactive learning, parents and educators can instill valuable financial habits in children, setting them on the path to a financially responsible and empowered future.

CHAPTER FOUR

EARNING AND BUDGETING

How Kids Can Earn Money

Teaching kids the value of money and the importance of financial responsibility is a vital aspect of their education. Encouraging children to earn their own money not only instills a sense of independence but also fosters valuable life skills. Here are some creative and age-appropriate ways for kids to earn money while having fun and learning valuable lessons along the way.

1. *Lemonade Stand Entrepreneurship*: Setting up a lemonade stand is a classic and time-tested way for kids to learn about business. From planning and budgeting to customer service, kids can grasp various aspects of entrepreneurship through this simple yet effective venture. They'll experience the joy of earning money while interacting with neighbors and enhancing their social skills.

2. *Pet Care Services*: Many families have pets, and kids can offer their services as pet sitters, dog walkers, or even pet groomers. Learning about animal care, responsibility, and time management, kids can establish a small neighborhood business that not only helps them earn

23

money but also provides a valuable service to their community.

3. *Yard Word and Gardening*: Helping neighbors with yard work, such as mowing lawns, raking leaves, or planting flowers, is another excellent way for kids to earn money. This not only teaches them the value of hard work but also allows them to enjoy the outdoors while contributing positively to their surroundings.

4. *Online Content Creation*: In the digital age, kids can explore opportunities in online content creation. Whether it's creating and selling digital art, starting a YouTube channel, or writing a blog, these activities can help kids develop their creativity, communication skills, and even a basic understanding of online marketing.

5. *Babysitting and Childcare*: For older kids who demonstrate responsibility and maturity, babysitting is a fantastic way to earn money while helping out parents in need. Obtaining basic first aid and childcare training can enhance their skills and give parents peace of mind.

6. *Crafts and handmade Goods*: Kids with a passion for crafting can turn their hobbies into a source of income. Creating handmade goods such as jewelry, custom greeting cards, or even DIY crafts to sell at local markets or online platforms provides

an opportunity for kids to express their creativity and entrepreneurship.

Empowering kids to earn money not only imparts financial literacy but also nurtures essential life skills such as responsibility, creativity, and communication. These experiences lay a foundation for a future generation that understands the value of hard work and the satisfaction of achieving their goals through effort and determination.

Budgeting Basics for Children
Teaching children about budgeting is a valuable life skill that lays the foundation for responsible financial habits. By instilling an early understanding of money management, parents can empower their children to make informed decisions and develop a healthy relationship with finances. We will now explore some fundamental concepts of budgeting tailored for children, making the learning process engaging and accessible.

1. *Introducing Money*: Begin by introducing the concept of money to children. Explain that money is a tool used to buy things and that it's earned through work or received as gifts. Share real-life examples to help them grasp the idea that money has value.
2. *Earning Money*: Teach children the importance of earning money through

chores, tasks, or even entrepreneurial ventures like a lemonade stand. This not only instills a sense of responsibility but also helps them understand the connection between effort and reward.

3. *Saving*: Emphasize the significance of saving money for future needs or wants. Introduce the concept of a savings jar or piggy bank, where they can deposit a portion of their earnings regularly. Encourage them to set short-term and long-term savings goals, making the process both practical and rewarding.

4. *Spending Wisely*: Teach children the difference between needs and wants. Help them prioritize their spending by discussing essential expenses versus optional purchases. Creating a simple spending plan or allowance system can provide a hands-on approach to managing their resources effectively.

5. *Budgeting Basics*: Introduce the concept of a budget as a tool for planning and managing money. Break down the budget into categories such as saving, spending, and sharing (charitable giving). Use relatable examples to demonstrate how budgeting ensures that there's enough money for different purposes.

6. *Tracking Expenses*: Encourage children to keep a record of their expenses, whether

on paper or using simple digital tools. This helps them understand where their money goes and facilitates informed decision-making about future spending.

7. *Making Choices*: Discuss the idea of making choices with limited resources. Present scenarios where they must decide between different options based on their budget constraints, fostering critical thinking and decision-making skills.

8. *Sharing and giving Back*: Instill the value of sharing and giving by allocating a portion of their budget for charitable purposes. Discuss the joy of helping others and the positive impact it can have on the community.

Teaching budgeting basics to children is an investment in their financial literacy and future success. By providing them with practical, age-appropriate lessons, parents can empower their children to navigate the world of finances with confidence and responsibility, setting the stage for a lifetime of informed money management.

Creating a Kid Friendly Budget

Teaching kids about money management is a valuable life skill that will serve them well in adulthood. One effective way to instill financial responsibility is by introducing them to the concept of a kid-friendly budget. By involving children in the budgeting process, parents can impart important lessons about saving, spending wisely, and making informed financial decisions. This passage will explore some practical tips and strategies for creating a kid-friendly budget that is both educational and enjoyable.

1. ***Start with the Basics***: Begin by explaining the fundamental concepts of budgeting in a simple and relatable manner. Define income, expenses, and savings, using age-appropriate language. Illustrate the idea of "money in" (allowance or income) versus "money out" (expenses and savings) to establish a foundational understanding.

2. ***Set Clear Goals***: Encourage children to identify short-term and long-term goals for their money. Whether it's saving for a new toy, a special outing, or even a more significant goal like a bike, having specific objectives helps kids understand the purpose of budgeting and saving.

3. ***Allocate Allowances***: Introduce the concept of an allowance as a form of income for kids. Discuss the importance of dividing their allowance into different categories, such as spending money, saving money, and perhaps even donating money to a cause they care about. This division helps them allocate funds responsibly.

4. **Create a Visual Budget**: Make the budget tangible by using visuals like charts or graphs. This could be a simple pie chart illustrating the percentage allocated to spending, saving, and giving. Visual aids can make the budgeting process more engaging and help kids grasp the distribution of their funds.

5. **Involve Them in Family Budget Discussions**: To provide a broader perspective, involve kids in age-appropriate discussions about the family budget. Explain how household expenses are managed and how decisions are made. This not only enhances their financial literacy but also fosters a sense of responsibility within the family unit.

6. **Encourage Smart Spending**: Teach kids about making informed choices when it comes to spending. Discuss the difference between needs and wants, and help them prioritize their purchases accordingly. Emphasize the importance of comparison shopping and looking for value in what they buy.

7. **Celebrate Achievements**: Celebrate small victories along the way, such as reaching a savings goal or making a thoughtful spending decision. Positive reinforcement helps children associate budgeting with

positive outcomes and encourages continued responsible financial behaviour.

Incorporating a kid-friendly budget into a child's upbringing is a powerful way to instill lifelong financial habits. By providing a hands-on experience, parents can empower their children to make informed financial decisions, setting the stage for a financially responsible future.

CHAPTER FIVE

NEEDS VS. WANTS: TEACHING KIDS ABOUT PRIORITIZING

Understanding Needs and Wants

Understanding needs and wants is an important aspect of a child's early development, laying the foundation for important life skills and values. Teaching kids to distinguish between their needs and wants not only fosters responsible decision-making but also helps them appreciate the value of resources and develop a sense of gratitude. Here's a passage to help children grasp the concept of needs and wants.

In the exciting adventure of growing up, children often encounter the concepts of needs and wants. Understanding the difference between these two is like having a special map that guides us through the journey of life. Let's embark on a discovery to unravel the mystery of needs and wants.

Imagine you are on a treasure hunt, and your treasure chest is filled with everything you require to live happily and healthily. These treasures are called "needs." They are the essentials, the must-haves that keep you strong, safe, and full of energy. What are some examples of needs? Well, the air we breathe, the water we drink, the food we eat, and the cozy shelter we call home are all part of this precious treasure.

Now, let's talk about "wants." Wants are like the glittery gems and shiny jewels you might find along the way. They are the things that make life more enjoyable but are not necessary for survival. Toys, games, and sweet treats are examples of wants. While these are fun to have, it's important to remember that our needs come first.

The challenge lies in the dynamic interplay between needs and wants, as they often intersect and evolve over time. While needs provide a foundation for survival and well-being, wants add depth and variety to our lives. Striking a balance between satisfying essential needs and pursuing reasonable wants is crucial for fostering a sense of contentment and avoiding the pitfalls of excessive consumption.

Understanding needs and wants also involves acknowledging the subjective nature of these concepts. What one person perceives as a need, another may view as a want, and vice versa. Cultural, economic, and individual differences contribute to the diversity of perspectives on what constitutes a need or a want.

Developing a nuanced understanding of needs and wants is essential for making informed choices, fostering personal well-being, and contributing to a sustainable and harmonious society. It requires introspection, awareness of societal influences, and the ability to prioritize what truly matters in the pursuit of a fulfilling and purposeful life.

Decision-Making Exercises
Helping children develop effective decision-making skills is crucial for their personal growth and future success. Decision-making exercises empower kids to think critically, consider consequences, and make informed choices. Through engaging and age-appropriate activities, children can enhance their decision-making abilities while having fun.

Exercise 1: The Choice Chart Objective: Teach children to weigh options and make decisions based on preferences.

Instructions:

1. Create a chart with two columns: "Option 1" and "Option 2."
2. Present children with simple choices, such as picking a game to play or a snack to eat
3. Have them list the pros and cons of each option in the respective columns
4. Encourage kids to reflect on their preferences and make a choice based on the information they gathered.

Exercise 2: Consequence Charades
Objective: Illustrate the concept of consequences and the impact of decisions.

Instructions:

1. Prepare a list of positive and negative consequences related to common decisions for kids (e.g., finishing homework on time, sharing toys, skipping chores).
2. Write each consequence on separate cards and place them in a bag.
3. Have children take turns choosing a card and acting out the consequence without revealing it verbally.
4. After the charade, discuss the decision that led to the consequence and why it happened.

Exercise 3: Decision Dilemmas Objective: Enhance critical thinking by presenting hypothetical scenarios for decision-making.

Instructions:

1. Create scenario cards describing everyday situations where a decision is required (e.g., choosing between playing outside and finishing homework).
2. Have children draw a scenario card and discuss the options available to them.

3. Encourage them to brainstorm alternative solutions and evaluate the potential outcomes.
4. Discuss as a group to share different perspectives on how the scenario could unfold.

Exercise 4: Decision Journal Objective: Foster self-reflection and awareness of decision-making patterns.

Instructions:

1. Provide children with a decision journal or notebook.
2. Ask them to record significant decisions they make each day, along with the thought process behind their choices.
3. Encourage reflection on the outcomes and feelings associated with each decision.
4. Discuss their entries periodically, offering guidance on improving decision-making skills based on past experiences.

By incorporating these decision-making exercises into children's routines, parents and educators can contribute to the development of vital life skills. These activities not only make the learning process enjoyable but also lay the foundation for responsible and thoughtful decision-making in the future.

CHAPTER SIX

BANKING FOR KIDS

Introduction to banks

Welcome to the exciting world of banks, where saving, spending, and learning about money become an adventure! Banks play a crucial role in our lives, and understanding how they work can be a fascinating journey for kids of all ages.

What is a Bank?

At its simplest, a bank is a special place that helps us manage our money. Just like a piggy bank at home, banks are safe places where we can keep our money and even earn a little extra. But banks do much more than just hold onto our coins and bills.

Saving Money: One of the coolest things about banks is that they help us save money. When you open a savings account, you're like a financial superhero. You put your money into the account, and the bank keeps it safe while also giving you something called "interest." Interest is like a reward for saving money - the more you save, the more interest you can earn

Making Money Grow: Imagine planting a seed in the ground and watching it grow into a big, strong tree. Banks can help your money grow, too! They offer special accounts, like a "piggy bank with wings," called a "savings account" or a "certificate of deposit." These accounts let your money grow over time, so when you need it later, you have even more than you started with.

Spending with Safety: Have you ever used a piggy bank to save money for something special? Well, banks have something similar called a "checking account." It's like a magic wallet that lets you safely spend your money. You can use checks, debit cards, or even online tools to pay for things without carrying around lots of cash.

Banks and Community: Banks aren't just about money; they're also about helping communities. They support local businesses, help people buy homes, and even provide loans for important things like education. When you put your money in a bank, you're helping your community grow and thrive!

Get ready to embark on an exciting journey to discover the secrets of banks, learn how money works, and become a financial wizard. Join us as we explore the world of savings, investments, and the incredible ways banks make our lives better!

Opening a Kid's Bank Account
Opening a kid's bank account is a crucial step in teaching financial responsibility and fostering good money habits from an early age. It provides

children with a practical and hands-on opportunity to learn about saving, budgeting, and the basics of banking. As parents, guardians, or caregivers embark on this financial journey with their young ones, there are several key considerations to keep in mind

First and foremost, it's essential to choose a bank that offers specialized accounts for children. Many financial institutions provide dedicated savings or youth accounts designed to cater to the unique needs of young account holders. These accounts often come with features such as low or no fees, a modest minimum balance requirement, and educational resources to help kids understand the fundamentals of money management

Before heading to the bank, take some time to explain the purpose and benefits of having a bank account to your child. Discuss concepts like earning interest, setting savings goals, and the security of keeping money in a bank. This initial conversation can help build excitement and a positive attitude towards financial responsibility.

When visiting the bank, be sure to bring all necessary documentation, including your child's social security number and proof of identity. Some banks may also require a minimum initial deposit, so it's wise to check the specific requirements beforehand. Take the opportunity to involve your child in the process by allowing them to interact with the bank staff, ask questions, and even make the initial deposit themselves.

Once the account is open, encourage your child to actively participate in managing their finances. Teach them how to keep track of their balance, make deposits, and set savings goals. Many banks offer online banking tools and mobile apps that can make this process more engaging for young account holders.

Opening a kid's bank account is not just a financial transaction; it's a valuable educational experience that lays the foundation for a lifetime of responsible money management. By instilling these financial skills early on, you empower your child to make informed decisions, cultivate a sense of independence, and develop a healthy relationship with money.

Using a Piggy Bank
In the journey of imparting essential life skills to children, financial responsibility ranks high on the list. One practical and time-tested tool that parents and guardians often use to instill the concept of saving in their young ones is the humble piggy bank. A piggy bank is not merely a container for loose change; it serves as a valuable tool for teaching children about money management, goal-setting, and the importance of delayed gratification.

Hands-on Learning: Introducing a piggy bank to a child provides a tangible and hands-on experience in handling money. The act of physically depositing coins or bills into the piggy bank allows children to understand the concrete value of currency and the significance of saving.

Basic financial Concepts: Piggy banks serve as excellent educational tools to teach children fundamental financial concepts such as saving, spending, and budgeting. By having a designated place to deposit money, kids can grasp the idea of setting aside funds for future needs or desired purchases.

Goal Setting: Encouraging children to set saving goals is an essential aspect of using a piggy bank. Whether it's saving for a favorite toy, a special outing, or even a long-term goal like a college fund, having a visual representation of their progress in the form of a filling piggy bank motivates kids to stick to their savings plans.

Delayed Gratification: The concept of delayed gratification is a valuable lesson that piggy banks can help instill. Instead of spending money impulsively, children learn to resist immediate desires and experience the satisfaction of achieving a goal through patience and perseverance.

Financial Literacy: Introducing a piggy bank at an early age lays the groundwork for future financial literacy. Children who grow up understanding the basics of money management are better equipped to make informed financial decisions as they mature into adults

Parental Involvement: Using a piggy bank is an excellent opportunity for parents and guardians to actively engage with their children on the topic of money. By discussing savings goals, celebrating milestones, and offering guidance on financial choices, parents can play a crucial role in shaping their child's financial habits.

In today's world of electronic transactions and digital wallets, the timeless piggy bank remains a powerful tool for teaching kids essential financial skills. By incorporating a piggy bank into a child's upbringing, parents and guardians contribute to their long-term financial well-being and nurture a sense of responsibility that will benefit them throughout their lives.

CHAPTER SEVEN

THE POWER OF COMPOUND INTEREST

Explaining Compound Interest in Simple Terms

Compound interest is a powerful financial concept that can significantly boost your savings over time. At its core, compound interest is like a magical snowball that grows as it rolls down a hill. Here's a simple breakdown to help you understand how it works.

Imagine you have some money, let's say $100, and you decide to put it in a savings account that offers compound interest. The bank pays you a certain percentage of interest on your initial $100, and here's where the magic begins.

In the first period, let's say the interest rate is 10%. So, you earn $10 in interest, making your total savings $110. Now, in the next period, the interest is calculated not just on your initial $100 but on the new total of $110. This means you earn $11 in interest this time, making your total savings $121.

The process continues, and with each period, you earn interest not just on your original amount but also on the interest you've already earned. This compounding effect creates a snowball effect, and over time, your money starts growing faster and faster.

The key takeaway is that compound interest allows your money to work for you, building on itself and accelerating your savings growth. The longer you leave your money invested, the more significant the impact of compound interest becomes. It's a simple yet powerful concept that highlights the importance of starting to save early and letting time work in your favour.

Fun Experiments to Demonstrate the Concept of Compound Interest

Compound interest is a financial concept that may sound complex, but its magic can be easily demonstrated through engaging and entertaining experiments. These activities not only make learning about compound interest enjoyable but also provide practical insights into its power over time. Whether you're a student, a parent, or simply curious about the wonders of finance, these fun experiments are sure to captivate and enlighten.

Experiment 1: The Penny-Doubling Game
Materials: A penny, a container, and a bit of patience.

Procedure:

1. Start with a single penny and place it in the container.
2. Double the number of pennies in the container every day.
3. Record the number of pennies and observe how quickly the amount grows

Explanation: This experiment mimics the compounding effect of interest over time. The initial penny represents the principal amount, and each day's doubling simulates the compounding process. As the days progress, the exponential growth of the pennies vividly illustrates the power of compound interest.

Experiment 2: The Investment Tree Materials: A paper tree template, colored markers, and stickers or cutouts of money symbols

Procedure:

1. Draw a tree with branches on a large piece of paper.
2. Label each branch with a different time period (e.g., 5 years, 10 years, 20 years).
3. On each branch, depict the growth of an investment over time using colorful markers and money symbols.

Explanation: This visual representation helps convey the idea that the longer money is invested, the more it grows. Each branch represents a specific time horizon, and the increasing number of money symbols on the branches illustrates the compounding effect of interest.

Experiment 3: The Savings Race Materials: A dice, a game board, and tokens representing savings.

Procedure:

1. Create a simple board with spaces representing different years.
2. Start with an initial savings amount (e.g., $100) and a goal amount.
3. Roll the dice to determine how much interest is earned each year and move the token accordingly.

Explanation: This interactive game simulates the journey of saving and investing over time. The randomness introduced by the dice adds an element of unpredictability, making it clear that while returns may vary, the longer the game (or investment period), the higher the chances of reaching the financial goal due to compound interest.

By engaging in these hands-on experiments, individuals of all ages can grasp the concept of compound interest in a playful and memorable way. Whether it's watching pennies multiply, creating visual representations of investment growth, or participating in a savings race, these activities demystify the power of compound interest, laying the foundation for a deeper understanding of financial concepts.

CHAPTER EIGHT

INVESTING FOR KIDS

Introduction to Investing

Welcome to the amazing world of investing, where your journey towards financial independence begins! This guide is tailored specifically for young minds eager to understand the basics of investing. Whether you're saving up for a special goal or just curious about how money grows, this introduction will lay the foundation for a lifetime of smart financial decisions.

Why Invest?

Investing is like planting seeds that grow into mighty trees over time. Just as you nurture a plant with water and sunlight, you can nurture your money by investing it wisely. Instead of stashing your allowance under the mattress, you can make it work for you by investing in things that have the potential to grow in value.

Understanding Money

Before we dive into the world of investing, let's take a moment to understand the concept of money. Money is a tool that allows us to buy things we need and want. However, instead of just spending it, you can make your money work for you by investing it. This means putting it into places where it can grow and earn more money over time.

What is Investing?

Investing is like being a part-owner of something. When you invest, you buy a share or a piece of something with the hope that it will become more valuable in the future. This could be a company, real estate, or other assets. By investing wisely, you can watch your money grow over the years.

Risk and Reward

Investing involves a degree of risk, just like any adventure. However, the good news is that you can learn to manage these risks. Think of it as choosing different paths on your journey – some may be more challenging, but they also offer greater rewards. Understanding the balance between risk and reward is a crucial part of becoming a successful investor.

Start Small, Dream Big

You don't need a fortune to start investing. In fact, starting small is a great way to learn and grow. As you gain more experience, you can increase your investments. The key is to be patient and let your money grow over time

In following pages we'll explore various investment options, such as stocks, bonds, and mutual funds. We'll also discover the importance of setting goals, creating a budget, and making informed decisions. So, fasten your seatbelt, young investor! Your financial adventure is about to begin, and with a little knowledge and patience, you'll be on your way to building a bright financial future.

Kids' friendly Investment Options

Investing for your child's future can be an exciting and rewarding way to set them up for financial success. While the world of finance may seem complex, there are kid-friendly investment options that can make the journey enjoyable and educational. Teaching children about the value of money and the power of saving early on can instill lifelong financial habits. Here are some fun and accessible investment options tailored for the young ones.

1. ***Piggy Banks and savings Accounts***:
   Start with the basics! Introduce the concept

of saving by giving your child a piggy bank. Watching loose change add up over time can be a simple yet effective lesson. As they grow, consider opening a savings account with them, providing an opportunity to learn about interest and the importance of setting financial goals.

2. *Educational Investment Apps*: Engage your child in the world of investing through kid-friendly apps designed to make learning about finances entertaining. These apps often use games and simulations to teach basic financial concepts, helping children understand the value of wise financial decisions.

3. *College Savings Plans*: Looking towards the future, a college saving plan is an excellent option for saving specifically for education expenses. These plans offer tax advantages and can be used for qualified educational expenses, making them a smart choice for parents who want to invest in their child's education from an early age.

4. *Stock Market Simulations*: Make learning about the stock market an exciting adventure! Many online platforms offer stock market simulations for children, allowing them to virtually invest in stocks without real money. This hands-on experience can help them understand the

basics of investing and the concept of risk and reward.

5. ***Custodial Investment Accounts***: For parents who want to invest on behalf of their children, custodial investment accounts provide a way to manage investments until the child reaches the age of majority. This option allows parents to guide investment decisions while teaching their children about the importance of long-term financial planning.

6. ***Treasury Securities***: Introduce your child to the world of government bonds! Treasury securities, such as savings bonds, are low-risk investments that are backed by the U.S. government. These can be a safe and educational way for kids to experience the concept of earning interest on their investments.

Teaching kids about financial responsibility and the world of investing can be an enjoyable and educational journey. By introducing them to kid-friendly investment options, parents can help instill a sense of financial literacy from an early age, setting the stage for a financially savvy future. Remember, the key is to make the process fun and interactive, allowing your child to learn valuable lessons about money while building a solid foundation for their financial future.

CHAPTER NINE

FINANCIAL RESPONSIBILITY AND CHORES

Linking Chores to Allowances

While raising responsible and financially savvy children, parents often grapple with the question of how to instill a strong work ethic and money management skills in their kids. One effective approach that many families adopt is linking chores to allowances. This method not only teaches children the value of hard work but also introduces them to the concept of earning and managing money from a young age.

1. ***Teaching Responsibility***: By assigning age-appropriate chores, parents can instill a sense of responsibility in their children. Basic tasks such as making the bed, tidying up their room, or setting the table not only contribute to the smooth functioning of the household but also teach kids the importance of taking care of their personal space and contributing to the well-being of the family.
2. ***Earning Through Effort***: Linking allowances to chores helps children understand that money is earned through effort and hard work. This valuable lesson

lays the foundation for a strong work ethic that will benefit them in their academic and later professional lives. It also reinforces the idea that rewards are tied to commitment and diligence.

3. *Money Management Skills*: As children earn their allowances, parents can seize the opportunity to teach essential money management skills. Encouraging them to save a portion of their earnings, allocate funds for specific purposes, and even budget for their wants versus needs provides practical financial education. These early lessons can set the stage for responsible financial habits in adulthood.

4. *Setting Goals*: Linking allowances to chores allows parents to introduce goal-setting to their children. Whether it's saving for a special toy, contributing to a charity, or planning for a future purchase, children learn the value of setting realistic goals and working towards achieving them. This experience fosters a sense of accomplishment and self-discipline.

5. *Fostering Independence*: As children take on responsibilities and manage their own allowances, they develop a sense of independence and autonomy. This empowerment is crucial for their personal development, as it encourages them to

make decisions, set priorities, and take ownership of their actions.

Linking chores to allowances is a powerful tool for parents aiming to raise responsible, independent, and financially literate children. Through this approach, children not only learn the value of hard work but also develop crucial life skills that will serve them well into adulthood. By creating a positive and educational connection between chores and allowances, parents contribute to the holistic development of their children, preparing them for a future of responsibility and financial competence.

Teaching Responsibility Through Tasks

Teaching responsibility is a vital aspect of a child's development, laying the foundation for lifelong skills and character traits. One effective way to instill a sense of responsibility in children is through engaging them in purposeful tasks. By assigning age-appropriate responsibilities, caregivers and educators can empower children to take ownership of their actions, cultivate independence, and develop a strong work ethic. This passage explores the importance of teaching responsibility through tasks and offers practical insights into implementing this approach.

The Power of Purposeful Tasks: Assigning tasks that contribute to the well-being of the family or classroom community can instill a sense of purpose in children. Simple chores such as setting the table, tidying up their play area, or watering plants not only teach responsibility but also foster a sense of belonging and pride in their contributions. Children begin to understand that their actions have a direct impact on those around them, promoting a positive and proactive mindset.

Gradual Progression: It is crucial to tailor tasks according to a child's age and abilities. Younger children may start with basic responsibilities like putting away toys, while older ones can take on more complex tasks such as preparing a simple snack or completing homework independently. Gradual progression ensures that children build confidence as they successfully accomplish tasks, setting the stage for more significant responsibilities in the future.

Setting Expectations and Consistency: Clear communication is essential when introducing tasks to children. Setting expectations and explaining the importance of their contributions helps children understand the purpose behind their responsibilities. Consistency in assigning and following through on tasks reinforces the idea that responsibility is an ongoing commitment. Establishing a routine also provides a sense of predictability, making it easier for children to integrate these responsibilities into their daily lives.

Encouraging Accountability: Encouraging children to take responsibility for their mistakes is a crucial aspect of the learning process. Rather than focusing on punitive measures, caregivers and educators can use mistakes as opportunities for growth. Discussing the consequences of actions and brainstorming solutions together helps children understand the connection between responsibility and accountability.

Celebrating Achievements: Positive reinforcement plays a pivotal role in reinforcing responsible behavior. Celebrate and acknowledge a child's efforts and accomplishments, no matter how small. This positive feedback reinforces the idea that responsibility is valued and appreciated, motivating children to continue taking on tasks with enthusiasm.

Teaching responsibility through purposeful tasks is a dynamic and rewarding process that contributes significantly to a child's overall development. By engaging children in age-appropriate responsibilities, caregivers and educators empower them to become responsible, self-reliant individuals who understand the impact of their actions on themselves and the world around them. Through this approach, we shape future generations with a strong foundation of responsibility, setting the stage for a lifetime of success and positive contributions to society.

CHAPTER TEN

MONEY AND TECHNOLOGY

The Role of Technology in Financial Management

The current technologically driven world has made financial literacy instruction for kids an important part of their education. The integration of technology into financial management for kids not only makes learning about money engaging but also equips them with crucial skills for a financially responsible future.

One of the primary ways technology contributes to financial education is through interactive apps and games designed specifically for children. These tools provide an entertaining and hands-on approach to learning basic financial concepts such as budgeting, saving, and responsible spending. Through colorful interfaces and gamified scenarios, kids can navigate virtual financial worlds, making decisions that mimic real-life financial scenarios.

Moreover, online platforms and apps offer parents the opportunity to introduce their children to the world of digital banking. Virtual savings accounts tailored for kids allow them to monitor their allowances, set savings goals, and even experience the concept of earning interest. Such platforms not only familiarize kids with the mechanics of banking but also teach them the importance of saving for future goals.

Technology also plays a crucial role in teaching kids about the digital currency landscape. With the rise of cryptocurrencies, it becomes essential for children to understand these concepts from an early age. Age-appropriate educational resources and games can demystify the complexities of digital currencies, fostering a basic understanding of this evolving aspect of the financial world.

Furthermore, online educational resources and video content contribute significantly to financial education for kids. Platforms offering animated videos and tutorials break down complex financial concepts into digestible, child-friendly content. This visual approach enhances comprehension and makes learning about money more enjoyable for young minds.

The integration of technology into financial management for kids serves as a powerful tool in shaping their financial future. Interactive apps, digital banking platforms, and educational resources provide a dynamic and engaging environment for children to learn essential financial skills. By harnessing the potential of technology, parents and educators can empower the next generation with the knowledge and confidence needed to navigate the complexities of personal finance responsibly.

Safe Online Money Management for Kids

In today's digital age, teaching kids about responsible online money management is an essential life skill. As children increasingly navigate the virtual world, it becomes crucial to instill good financial habits early on. By providing guidance and establishing a secure foundation, parents can empower their children to make informed decisions and develop a healthy relationship with money. Here are some key principles for safe online money management for kids:

1. *Education and Communication*: Begin by educating children about the concept of money, its value, and the importance of responsible financial behavior. Foster open communication, encouraging them to ask questions and share their thoughts about money matters. Use age-appropriate language to explain basic financial concepts, such as saving, spending, and budgeting.

2. *Secure Online Platforms*: Emphasize the importance of using secure and reputable online platforms for money-related activities. Introduce children to child-friendly banking apps or websites designed

specifically for kids, ensuring these platforms prioritize safety and privacy. Avoid sharing sensitive information online and teach them to recognize trustworthy websites.

3. **Setting Financial Goals**: Help children establish realistic financial goals, whether it's saving for a specific toy, game, or future expenses. Break down larger goals into smaller, achievable milestones to make the process more manageable. This not only teaches them the value of setting objectives but also cultivates patience and discipline.

4. **Budgeting Basics**: Introduce the concept of budgeting by explaining the difference between needs and wants. Teach kids to allocate their money wisely, dividing it into categories such as saving, spending, and giving. Encourage them to prioritize their spending based on their goals and necessities.

5. **Monitoring and Tracking**: Teach children to monitor their online transactions regularly. Show them how to keep track of their expenses and savings, providing them with a sense of financial responsibility. Monitoring online activities not only promotes awareness but also helps in identifying and addressing any unauthorized or unusual transactions.

6. **_Parental Involvement_**: Maintain an active role in your child's financial education. Regularly discuss their financial activities, review their progress, and offer guidance when needed. By staying involved, parents can address any concerns early on and reinforce positive money management habits.
7. **_Online Safety Awareness:_** Emphasize the importance of online safety, including the need for strong and unique passwords. Teach children about the risks associated with sharing personal information online and the potential consequences of engaging in unsafe financial practices.
8. **_Critical thinking skills_**: Encourage the development of critical thinking skills when it comes to making financial decisions. Discuss scenarios where they might need to evaluate options, compare prices, and consider the long-term impact of their choices.

By incorporating these principles into a child's financial education, parents can lay the groundwork for responsible and safe online money management. Empowering children with the knowledge and skills to navigate the digital financial landscape prepares them for a future where financial literacy is an invaluable asset.

CHAPTER ELEVEN

FINANCIAL ROLE MODELS

The Influence of Parents and Guardians

The influence of parents and guardians on the development of a child is profound and enduring, shaping the foundation of their character, values, and overall well-being. From the earliest moments of infancy to the formative years of adolescence, the role played by parents and guardians is pivotal in sculpting the future trajectory of their children's lives.

In the realm of emotional development, parents serve as the primary architects of a child's sense of security and self-worth. The warmth, affection, and responsiveness displayed by caregivers create a nurturing environment that fosters emotional resilience and a healthy sense of attachment. This emotional foundation becomes the cornerstone upon which children build their relationships with others and navigate the complexities of the social world.

Furthermore, parents are instrumental in instilling moral values and ethical principles in their offspring. Through both explicit teachings and subtle modeling of behavior, parents shape the moral compass of their children. The values transmitted within the familial context serve as a compass that guides individuals throughout their lives, influencing decision-making, interpersonal relationships, and contributions to society.

Educationally, parents play a crucial role in fostering a love for learning and intellectual curiosity. The home environment serves as an initial classroom where children acquire fundamental skills, attitudes, and a thirst for knowledge. The encouragement, expectations, and involvement of parents in their child's educational journey significantly impact academic achievement and set the stage for a lifelong pursuit of learning.

Moreover, parents serve as the first and most influential role models for their children. Beyond shaping beliefs and values, they exemplify important life skills, work ethic, and resilience in the face of challenges. Children often emulate the behaviors and attitudes of their parents, internalizing these traits as they navigate their own paths.

In the ever-evolving landscape of personal and professional development, parents and guardians act as lifelong guides. Their support and guidance during critical transitional phases, such as career choices and major life decisions, can profoundly impact the trajectory of their children's lives.

The influence of parents and guardians is multifaceted, encompassing emotional, moral, educational, and role-modeling dimensions. The impact of their guidance extends far beyond the formative years, shaping the very essence of who their children become. Recognizing the significance of this influence underscores the responsibility and privilege inherent in the role of parenting, emphasizing the potential to positively shape the future through intentional and supportive caregiving.

Encouraging Responsible Financial Behaviour

In a world that increasingly revolves around financial literacy, instilling responsible financial behavior in children from a young age is crucial. Teaching kids about money early on not only equips them with essential life skills but also sets the foundation for a lifetime of sound financial decision-making. Here are some key strategies to encourage responsible financial behavior in children:

1. *Start Early*: Introduce basic financial concepts to children as soon as they can grasp the idea of money. Use everyday situations like shopping to explain the value of coins and bills, and involve them in simple transactions to build their understanding.

2. ***Set an Example***: Children often learn by observing their parents and caregivers. Demonstrate responsible financial behavior by budgeting, saving, and making informed spending choices. Discuss your financial decisions with them, helping them understand the rationale behind each choice.

3. ***Establish a Saving Habit***: Encourage the habit of saving by providing a piggy bank or a savings account. Help children set realistic savings goals for items they desire, emphasizing the satisfaction that comes from patiently saving and achieving those goals.

4. ***Teach budgeting Skills***: Introduce the concept of budgeting by assigning allowances and helping children allocate funds for different purposes. This not only teaches them to prioritize spending but also instills the importance of planning ahead.

5. ***Discuss Needs Vs Wants***: Differentiating between needs and wants is a fundamental aspect of responsible financial behavior. Engage in conversations about the necessity of certain expenses versus discretionary spending, fostering a mindset that values financial prudence.

6. ***Involve Kids in Family Finance***: As children grow older, involve them in discussions about family finances. Share

age-appropriate information about income, expenses, and financial goals. This transparency helps them develop a realistic understanding of the financial responsibilities that come with adulthood.

7. *Introduce Basic Investing Concepts*: As children mature, introduce them to basic investing concepts. Discuss the power of compound interest and the potential benefits of long-term investing, planting the seeds for a future understanding of wealth building.

8. *Encourage Entrepreneurial Thinking*: Foster creativity and entrepreneurial spirit by supporting children in exploring ways to earn money. Whether through a lemonade stand, chores, or other age-appropriate ventures, this experience instills a sense of initiative and work ethic.

9. *Promote Charitable Giving*: Teach children the value of generosity and responsible citizenship by incorporating charitable giving into their financial education. Encourage them to donate a portion of their allowances or earnings to causes they care about.

10. *Provide Guidance, Not Control:* While offering guidance is essential, allow children to make some financial decisions on their own. Mistakes can be valuable learning experiences, and giving them

autonomy helps build confidence in their financial decision-making abilities.

By incorporating these strategies into a child's upbringing, parents and caregivers play a pivotal role in shaping responsible financial behavior. Building a strong foundation of financial literacy during childhood sets the stage for a future generation of financially savvy and responsible adults.

CHAPTER TWELVE

DEALING WITH MONEY MISTAKES

Learning From Financial Errors

While growing up, kids are faced with numerous opportunities to learn and make choices, and one important aspect of life that deserves attention early on is money management. Teaching children about financial literacy is a valuable gift that will empower them to make informed decisions and set the stage for a secure future. One essential lesson in this financial education is the ability to learn from financial errors.

Mistakes are a natural part of life, and the world of finances is no exception. By making age-appropriate financial decisions and facing the consequences, kids can develop a deeper understanding of money and cultivate responsible habits. Here are some key lessons children can learn from financial errors:

1. ***Budgeting Basics***: Mistakes often occur when kids don't have a clear understanding of budgeting. Encouraging them to create a simple budget for their allowances or earnings helps instill the importance of planning and prioritizing expenses. When they overspend in one area, they can see

first-hand the impact on the rest of their budget.

2. ***Delayed Gratification***: Impulse spending is a common financial pitfall. Kids can learn about delayed gratification by setting savings goals for items they want. If they make the mistake of spending their money impulsively, they'll experience the delayed joy of achieving their goals, teaching them the value of patience and discipline.

3. ***Evaluating Choices***: Financial errors offer an opportunity for kids to reflect on their choices. Did they prioritize their needs over wants? Did they consider alternative options before making a purchase? Evaluating these choices helps them develop critical thinking skills that extend beyond the realm of money.

4. ***Saving for the Unexpected***: Unexpected expenses are a part of life, and kids can learn the importance of having an emergency fund. If they experience a financial setback, such as losing a toy or damaging an item, it becomes a chance to discuss the significance of saving for unforeseen circumstances.

5. ***Learning to Adapt***: Financial mistakes provide a valuable lesson in adaptability. Children can learn to reassess their financial plans, make adjustments, and develop resilience in the face of

unexpected challenges. These skills will serve them well as they navigate the complexities of adulthood.

Learning from financial errors is a crucial part of a child's financial education. By allowing them to make mistakes in a controlled environment, we equip them with the skills and mindset necessary for sound financial decision-making. These early lessons become building blocks for a future where they can confidently manage their finances, make informed choices, and achieve their long-term goals.

Developing a Healthy Attitude Towards Setbacks

In the journey towards cultivating financial intelligence in children, it is imperative to recognize the pivotal role that setbacks play in their development. Building a healthy attitude towards setbacks is not only crucial for financial literacy but also for fostering resilience, adaptability, and a positive mindset. Teaching children how to navigate setbacks empowers them with essential life skills that extend far beyond their financial endeavors.

Setbacks are an inevitable part of any learning process, and financial education is no exception. Whether it's a minor financial miscalculation or a more significant challenge, these setbacks provide invaluable opportunities for children to learn and grow. Instead of shielding them from financial realities, parents and educators should embrace setbacks as teachable moments that contribute to a well-rounded financial education.

One key aspect of developing a healthy attitude towards setbacks is reframing failure as a stepping stone to success. Children need to understand that setbacks are not indicative of their worth or abilities; rather, they are opportunities to reassess, learn, and improve. Encouraging a growth mindset instills in them the belief that their abilities can be developed through dedication and hard work, a mindset that is fundamental to financial success.

Furthermore, parents and educators play a crucial role in creating a supportive environment that encourages open communication about setbacks. By fostering an atmosphere where children feel comfortable discussing their financial challenges, they are more likely to seek guidance and learn from their experiences. This open dialogue allows for the imparting of practical financial wisdom and the development of problem-solving skills.

It is essential to introduce children to the concept of financial goals early on and help them understand that setbacks are not roadblocks but detours on the path to achieving these objectives. This perspective instills resilience and perseverance, qualities that are invaluable in navigating the complexities of personal finance throughout their lives.

Developing a healthy attitude towards setbacks is integral to nurturing kids' financial intelligence. By reframing setbacks as opportunities for growth, fostering a growth mindset, and creating an open dialogue, parents and educators can empower children with the skills and mindset needed to navigate the intricate world of finances. In doing so, we not only equip them with the tools for financial success but also lay the foundation for a resilient and adaptable approach to life's challenges.

CHAPTER THIRTEEN

CHARITY AND GIVING

Teaching Kids About Charity and Giving Back

Instilling financial intelligence in children goes beyond teaching them about budgeting and conserving money in a society that frequently prioritizes material success. It involves imparting values that extend beyond personal gain and towards the greater good of society. One powerful way to achieve this is by teaching kids about charity and the importance of giving back

Children are naturally curious and compassionate beings, making them receptive to lessons about empathy and generosity. Introducing the concept of charity at an early age not only cultivates a sense of social responsibility but also lays the foundation for financial intelligence. Here's how parents and educators can incorporate these principles into a child's learning journey:

1. **Lead by Examples**: Children often learn by observing the behavior of those around them. Parents and teachers can serve as role models by actively engaging in charitable activities. Whether it's volunteering at a local shelter, participating in community clean-ups, or supporting a

charitable cause, demonstrating these actions instills the importance of giving back.

2. ***Hands-On Experience***: Instead of just talking about charity, provide children with hands-on experiences. Encourage them to actively participate in charitable events or initiatives. This could include organizing a food drive, collecting toys for underprivileged children, or participating in a charity run. Through direct involvement, children can witness the positive impact of their contributions.

3. ***Setting Financial Goals for Giving***: Teach children the value of earmarking a portion of their allowances or earnings for charitable purposes. Help them set specific financial goals for giving back, emphasizing that even small contributions can make a difference. This not only instills the habit of budgeting but also reinforces the idea that financial success is not solely about personal accumulation.

4. ***Educate on Social Issues***: Introduce age-appropriate discussions about social issues and the disparities that exist in the world. This could include conversations about poverty, hunger, or environmental concerns. By fostering an understanding of these challenges, children develop a

heightened sense of empathy and a desire to contribute towards positive change.

5. ***Create a Giving Plan***: Encourage children to create a giving plan, outlining how they intend to allocate their charitable funds. This process involves thoughtful consideration of various causes and organizations. By researching and selecting causes that resonate with them, children gain a deeper understanding of the impact their contributions can have on the world.

6. ***Reflect on Impact***: After engaging in charitable activities, take the time to reflect with children on the impact of their efforts. Discuss how their contributions have made a difference and how they feel about being a part of positive change. This reflection reinforces the connection between financial choices and their broader impact on society.

By integrating these principles into a child's upbringing, parents and educators contribute to the development of financially intelligent individuals who not only understand the importance of managing resources but also appreciate the profound impact of generosity on the well-being of others and society as a whole.

Involving Children in Philanthropic Activities

Financial literacy has become essential to children's general development in a world where materialism and consumerism rule the day. While traditional approaches focus on savings, budgeting, and investment, an innovative avenue to impart financial acumen involves engaging children in philanthropic activities. By integrating philanthropy into their lives, children not only develop a sense of empathy and social responsibility but also gain valuable insights into financial management, creating a foundation for a financially intelligent future.

1. *Building Empathy and Social Responsibility*: Encouraging children to participate in philanthropic activities introduces them to the diverse needs of society. Whether it's volunteering at a local charity, participating in community projects, or contributing to a social cause, children learn to empathize with others and understand the impact of their actions on the community. This early exposure fosters a sense of social responsibility, a cornerstone of financial intelligence.

2. *Understanding Resource Allocation*: Philanthropic endeavors often involve the allocation of resources, be it time, money, or effort. Engaging children in the decision-

making process of where to direct these resources helps them comprehend the concept of resource allocation. This hands-on experience teaches them to make thoughtful choices, a skill directly applicable to financial decision-making later in life.

3. *Budgeting and Planning*: Many philanthropic activities require a budget and planning, mirroring real-world financial scenarios. Children, when involved in fundraising for a cause or organizing events, learn the importance of budgeting, setting financial goals, and planning for effective resource utilization. These experiences lay the groundwork for budgeting skills that are essential for personal finance management.

4. *Teamwork and Collaboration*: Philanthropy often involves collaboration and teamwork. Children working together towards a common goal learn the value of cooperation and shared responsibility. These collaborative experiences contribute to their ability to navigate financial partnerships, negotiate financial decisions, and understand the significance of collective financial efforts.

5. *Long-Tearm Impact and Sustainability*: Engaging in philanthropy exposes children to the long-term impact of financial decisions. They witness how sustained

efforts can lead to positive, lasting change. This perspective encourages a forward-thinking approach to financial planning, emphasizing the importance of sustainability and strategic financial decisions that contribute to long-term well-being.

Involving children in philanthropic activities serves as a dynamic and holistic approach to fostering financial intelligence. Beyond the conventional teachings of saving and investing, philanthropy provides children with practical experiences that shape their understanding of empathy, responsibility, resource allocation, teamwork, and long-term impact. By integrating these values into their financial education, we empower children to become financially astute individuals who not only manage their finances wisely but also contribute meaningfully to the well-being of the society they inhabit.

CHAPTER FOURTEEN

FINANCIAL LITERACY GAMES

Educational Games and Apps

Technology has emerged as a powerful ally in shaping the learning journey of young minds. Educational games and apps designed for kids have become invaluable tools, seamlessly blending entertainment with knowledge acquisition. These interactive platforms serve as engaging gateways to a world where learning is not just a task but a thrilling adventure.

1. ***Learn Through Play***: Educational games for kids transcend the traditional classroom setting, offering a dynamic learning experience through play. Whether solving puzzles, embarking on virtual quests, or engaging in interactive storytelling, these games stimulate a child's cognitive abilities, problem-solving skills, and creativity. The integration of educational content within a playful context makes the learning process enjoyable and fosters a love for exploration and discovery.

2. ***Personalized Learning Paths***: One of the greatest advantages of educational apps is their ability to tailor learning experiences to individual needs. These platforms adapt to a child's pace, allowing them to progress at

their own speed and revisit concepts as needed. Personalized feedback and adaptive learning algorithms ensure that each child receives targeted support, reinforcing strengths and addressing weaknesses. This customization enhances the efficacy of the learning journey, making it more meaningful and impactful.

3. ***Multisensory Engagement***: Educational games and apps leverage the multisensory nature of interactive media, catering to various learning styles. Incorporating visuals, auditory cues, and hands-on interactions, these tools provide a holistic learning experience. By appealing to different senses, they reinforce concepts and accommodate diverse learning preferences, ensuring that every child can grasp and retain information effectively.

4. ***Real World Application:*** Many educational games and apps bridge the gap between theoretical knowledge and real-world application. Through simulations and virtual scenarios, children can explore and apply what they've learned in a context that mirrors the complexities of everyday life. This practical approach fosters critical thinking skills, decision-making abilities, and a deeper understanding of how academic concepts relate to the world around them.

5. ***Parental Involvement and Progress Tracking:*** Educational apps often incorporate features that facilitate parental involvement in a child's learning journey. Parents can monitor progress, track achievements, and gain insights into their child's strengths and areas for improvement. This collaborative aspect strengthens the parent-child-teacher triad, fostering a supportive learning environment that extends beyond the classroom.

Educational games and apps for kids have revolutionized the educational landscape by turning learning into an exciting and immersive experience. These tools not only supplement traditional teaching methods but also pave the way for a more personalized, engaging, and effective approach to education. As technology continues to advance, the potential for educational games and apps to shape the future of learning remains boundless, offering endless possibilities for young minds to thrive in a world of knowledge and discovery. As parents and educators, one powerful tool at our disposal is literature. Engaging books (hard copies, audio and e-books) can make the complex concepts of finance accessible and enjoyable for children.

CONCLUSION

"Financial Intelligence for Kids" not only equips young minds with the essential tools for navigating the complex world of finances but also lays the foundation for a lifetime of informed and responsible decision-making. By instilling the principles of financial intelligence early on, this guide empowers children to become architects of their own financial destinies, fostering a generation capable of turning dreams into realities and aspirations into achievements. The guide also provide parents and educators the resource with which they can instill the principles of financial intelligence in children. As we close the chapters of this enlightening journey, let us celebrate the knowledge gained, the skills honed, and the seeds of financial acumen planted in the fertile minds of our youth. May the lessons learned here serve as a compass, guiding them towards a future where financial prowess becomes a cornerstone of their success and fulfillment. With each turn of the page, we witness the transformation of young minds into savvy stewards of their financial destinies, ensuring a legacy of prosperity, resilience, and wisdom.

Be Financially Intelligent!